Acknowledgments

Thank you to my mother, who claims to be the genetic source of my 'writing talent', and to my father, who asserts the same. Much love to my sister, Carol; my godmother, Nee Nee; all of my extended family; and my best friend, Rae.

Sincerest gratitude to the writers and artists who helped me to imagine, revise, publish, package and promote this book: Patience Agbabi, Dr. Jan Fortune, Dr. Richard Gwyn, Dr. Joyce Hinnefeld, Dr. Holly Howitt, Non Prys Ifans, Chris McGinnis, Nathan Meyer, Helia Phoenix and Dave Summers.

Special recognition to the editors and publishers of these anthologies and journals for publishing current or earlier versions of my poems: *A Roof of Red Tiles:* "A Man's Abortions," "Embers," "Painkiller" (Cinnamon Press, 2011); *Assaracus*, Issue 08: "David Poseidon," "The Hush," "Memory Hits," "Songbird," "World Wide Web" (Sibling Rivalry Press, 2012); *Exposure:* "Exposure," "Grace," "Pick-up Line," "Piñata" (Cinnamon Press, 2010); *Glimmer*: "Bazaar," "Nové," "Williamette" (Cinnamon Press, 2010); *In The Telling*: "Journey," "Meltdown" (Cinnamon Press, 2009); *The Review of Contemporary Poetry*: "The Girl Who Broke New Ground" (Bluechrome, 2005); *Sentence: A Journal of Prose Poetics*, Issue 09: "Word Problem" (Firewheel Editions, 2012); *Your Messages*: "Skeleton Key," "Unblink, Unclench" (Bluechrome, 2008).

Contents

For my heroes,
William J. and Diana,
and their heroes,
William Edward Trüb and Rose Marinelli

All Men Are Afraid

Pick-up Line

Just wondering if you'd like to grab some beers sometime, maybe at Duplex down on Christopher Street or anywhere this side of the International Date Line, wherever singles splash conversation like anvils introducing themselves to puddles with strangers whose names are lost in the bottoms of pint glasses then found between twin sheets; people who tell their life histories in one breath but can't tell a tree trunk from a toothpick, a traveler from a tourist, a man from a man; people like you and me who only like people like you and me: Scorpios in the sky, Scorpios in the sack, love-foolish jacks aspiring to be kings of a heartless deck, still wondering if, maybe, we could shed our muscles and make-up long enough to make sense of ourselves.

Men

Maybe he's lobotomized, party hat
askew on that bald case keeping
his brain from spilling out like a squid

or maybe he's tequila tipsy, downing
shooters at The Cock on 2nd Ave.
can make a tough guy fight a mirror

or maybe he survived that open heart
surgery when his arteries doubled
as copper pipes at age 39 and two halves

or maybe he lugs sadness in lavender bags
under his eyes and with each bastard blink
he's horrified by the encroaching beasts

or maybe his backpacking days are done
and his life is a bland riot of paper clips
and protein powder, reality TV and debt

or maybe he fisted a trumpet
and practiced unsafe sax until jazz
stained his satin sheet music

or maybe he's an eager sharpshooter
with his arrows in a row and his target's
the shrink slowly driving him sane

or maybe he kissed a man he thought
was a woman in a world he thought
was fair on a day he thought was perfect.

Liars

Jeremiah said, 'I'm homeless and it's my 24th birthday,' so I took him to my apartment. I was drunk and that's a good excuse.

He slept in paisley boxer shorts, the elastic waistband irreversibly stretched. Small, brown nipples, tight abdomen, hairless body. Ropes for arms, rockslides for legs. He snored like a small girl.

I went through his bag and found his driver's license in a sock. It was not his birthday, he was not 24 and his name was not Jeremiah.

'Dude, wake up.' I pretended his belly button was Eject and pressed it. 'I got things to do today like sleep alone and make lists.'

He walked out of my apartment in his boxers. From the stoop, he yelled up to my window, 'Hey Antonio, you got a Metrocard so I don't gotta jump the turnstile?'

I dropped the blinds and slid his license under my mattress with all of the others.

A Man's Abortions

In 1981, he fell out of his mother
and pattered feverish zigzags
into the carpet. In 1983, he formed
neon nouns in his mouth. In 1990,
he invented invisibility

and no one saw him for a decade.
In 2001, overweight yet starving,
he got a job at The Boredom Store.
His ears curved like question marks.
Light bulb: He tried to be a she

but his manhood was stronger
than the snip. In 2003, he married
and lost 6-0, 6-0, 6-0. Thumbs up,
he hitchhiked 3,000 miles across
a scatter of violent, untied states

to California. There, wildfires raged
between his temples until he stopped
mistaking people for peepholes
and trying to see through them.
In 2008, he ran against Jesus

for president of the universe
and they both lost to a pretty
dumb Alaskan. So he gave an STI
to the Internet and misinformation
inflamed every voter's fat head.

In 2009, while living out of bags,
he decided to think inside the box:
He stole steel, built a time capsule
and stuffed it with unfinished business,
an archive of a man's abortions,

a timeline of trophies and atrophies,
oopsie daisies and oh shits. In 2014,
when the world opened it, he hid
like a proud arsonist and watched
no one, save his mom, understand.

Unblink, Unclench

I

Son, find me in black and white
circa 1986. You hold the negative
of a photograph in front of a lamp—you glow
atop my shoulders. 'Who's my best bud?'
Your small voice chirps, 'Me!'

I remember throwing quick punches
centimeters from your face, so fast
the motion fluttered your bangs.
Your old man was a boxer before he was a father.

Son, let's meet halfway in a shared dream.
Maybe in Hope, NJ at The Land of Make Believe.
Maybe there, we could ride a roller coaster
with so many ups and downs our past will seem serene.

Maybe we need an amusement park to teach us to laugh.

Son, there's a stockpile of masks we've worn
to act like dunces, scholars, traitors and titans.
Our characters spoke dangerous gibberish
and only opened their eyes when alone.

Let's unblink for a moment and recognize each other.

II

Dad, you mean the world to me
and it won't end because you suck
jugs of Cabernet or because I've enjoyed
a few good men, some older than you.

We search for each other in our vices.
Our consciences shake us awake at 4am,
make us lead-headed, pillow-hungry zombies.

Dad, let's meet halfway in a shared dream.
Maybe in a palace in Baghdad. Maybe there,
apologies sound like meadowlarks.
Maybe we'd get more bang for our buck,
more body bags for us to tow to the Tigris
our rumbles of the past and finally sink them.

Maybe we need a war zone to recognize a tiff.

Dad, there's a great man locked in my head.
It's your blind father, tapping a Braille pocket watch,
reminding me that hindsight is 20/20 and obese
with regret, but foresight is a cure-all in our palms.

Let's unclench our fists and find it.

Windmilled

I used to glare at the beggar
who sat by the cash point on Queen Street in Cardiff
and asked people to spare twenty pence until one night
I saw a pigeon with pizza crust in its beak fly past
and the beggar windmilled his good arm

and I swear he knocked the bird right out of the fucking air

and ran off with the crust
and I swear this is exactly what happened
except the pigeon was my face
and the crust was my wallet
and the beggar was Grandma Jane
who I thought was buried in America
but I could be wrong.

I Stutter

because a mockingbird
is perched on my tongue
and when I split my lips
to spit a sentence, it blitzes
the hole. I slam my mouth shut
mid-word and, beak-first,
it crashes into the back of an eye
tooth. It wants to glide
on a prick of a breeze
and sing the secrets
I thought I swallowed.

I take it like a man—
one hard gulp,
guttural cough,
swirl of feathers,
the slowing flap
of wings in my stomach.

Journey

West inside the belly of a boy, east
echoes in his ears, north is a lift drifting
up his spine, south sails his waistline.

Open-faced every Monday morning,
closed-minded by Friday's morphing
into a wreck of weekend, he sleeps

dreamlessly on a strand of Barcelona,
awakes barefooted, tale on his tongue,
fresh bite mark in his passport.

Unmarried to a flag, he glides on rails
in a second-class carriage, a determined dusk
grows into midnight, a tarp atop Spain.

Soon behind him colors rise, orange
burns through a gloom-grey sky, he speaks
Catalan in stutters to a stranger in the sea.

He smells the perfume of a fish market,
a woman wraps snapper in *El Pais*, a girl
dribbles a football around a fruit stand.

He traps this scene inside his skull.
Later, he'll build stanzas like castles
of sand then watch them wash away.

But there's a journal in his rucksack
kept only for himself. And there's a cloud
that opens in his head sometimes

and, sometimes, he fattens the albatross
around his neck with sticks of chocolate
and the journey means more.

The World Doesn't End

Called 'Little Paris' in a time when things mattered, Neve Tzedek
is a crush of peeling, once whitewashed walls lost in Tel Aviv.
Gates are rusted shut; ivy smatters archways like a virus. I drag
my suitcase down an alley.

A green door is the only splash of paint. The knocker: a brass
lioness chomping a ring. I palm its face and push.

One room. Dazzle of light, cubed. I drop my luggage and notice
the walls. Flesh-toned. Pores, arm hair, acne—all familiar hides
I've worn. A range of pigments tailored around window sills and
the light switch, edged beneath crown molding. On the ceiling I
discover a collection of clock faces—hour and minute hands
spread-eagled. These were my expiration dates.

In a drawer: photographs of an infant leeching a breast, a kid in
an iron lung, an old man with his head in his hands. In a shoebox:
wooden dentures, Olympic gold, two bullets. On a bookshelf:
Simic's *The World Doesn't End*.

On the radio: the scattershot of Björk's 'Hunter' decomposes into
'Real Men' by Joe Jackson. I smell burning buildings, the spices of
Sichuan, freshly mown suburbia. Through three windows I see
one landscape, one seascape and one great escape.

I sit on the floor and absorb my pasts. When the gilded cat on the
green door roars, I know it's time to leave. I zip my suitcase,
paunchy now, and fold the wallpaper precisely into thirds. Then
down into sixths, a roadmap.

Ready?

The day pulls on a faded hoodie from college. Birds listen to chirps on their iPods. A black and white rainbow flatlines above the city. I adjust my shoulder straps.

Life: reluctant, hungover, slo-mo. I sip tap water and consider opening the curtains, but don't. The air in my apartment is odorless. Family and friends are frozen in frames. While I brainstorm excuses to be late for work, my cell phone vibrates and scares the shit out of me.

Yo! Was thinking about you and wanted to say hi. Let's hang out soon.

Pause, then a second blast.

Actually DO something though, not just talk about it. I'm in Brooklyn a lot. Let's jump off the bridge.

He's younger than I am but better at being an adult. Years ago, I gave him a treasure chest filled with sand from the Sahara, pence from Britain, seashells from the Jersey Shore. And a note which read: *You're the only one who can create an adventurous life for yourself.*

Years later, he boarded an airplane, clipped its wings and crashed in a different era. I don't know what he did there but, when he returned, he gave me a parachute and told me to put it on.

Venus Fly Traps

'May I join?' She slung her pack onto the bottom berth diagonal to me. I passed down my bottle of red. She slugged then unwrapped a small block of Muenster from a handkerchief. She quartered it with a pocket knife and handed two chunks to me. A wisp of human, as if half mantis. But her eyes: pea-green, crumbs of umber and full, slaphappy lashes.

Italy spilt into Slovenia beneath the ink. We drained the wine as the old train trudged east. She was traveling to the Julian Alps for an art installation. 'I reuse things people throw away. Car parts, dishes, lampshades, then I create.' With a giggle, 'Just a woman from Berlin who collects rubbish.'

I told her I was going to Ljubljana to perform at a festival. 'There's a bridge bookended by dragons in the city center. Jugglers, dancers, rappers. That's where I'll rhyme.'

She swept her fringe from her face. 'What do you write about?'

'Fucked up relationships,' I said. 'Between humans and places, father and son, man and society, man and man.' I was wasted by this point, drinking since Verona. 'But the most important thing to remember when you write is that no one cares what you have to say.'

She turned away, unwound her scarf. 'This train has ears. We have said too much.' Fragile-faced, she turned back to me. A meaty, pink scar ran horizontally across her neck.

'What's your name?' I said, startled sober.

She unrolled her sleeping bag. 'Elisa Hoff. Yours?'

22

'Bill Trüb.'

She exhaled onto the cold window and pointed at the fog. 'Your surname.'

She watched me as she moved to her bunk. I could see myself in her pupils. When her head met the mattress, her eyelids snapped shut. Her lashes interlocked.

The Exchange

A souk in Sousse. Market men haggle in French, hock Berber rugs
and sand roses, horned vipers in glass cases, hookahs and
sharmutas. A tourist turns a rack of postcards while a boy
pickpockets him. I elbow through the mob. Voices clutter like
souvenirs. A Mediterranean breeze brings the fiasco from
Carthage and the boy is gone.

A woman swathed in black fabric, beaded with sweat, groans
beneath an extremist sun. She's selling CDs. I drop two dinars
into her lap; her mouth crumples into a smile snagged by tusks. I
wonder where she lives and if she has children. I say, 'Merci
beaucoup.' She thumbs the gold coins and belches.

I never listened to the disc until now, nine years later, as I sit in a
Brooklyn loft and pluck greys from my scalp. I press play: snake
of Arabic, tabla beats, tambourine shakes and scribbles of lute. It
skips as I shoot back to that holiday in Tunisia where I
photographed the privileged and the poor, shoveled couscous
into my mouth and lost my virginity to the entire world at once.

Cosmosis

Small village, big mountain. Mogodumo, two hours from the Zimbabwean border. It's 3am. Electricity has been down since 6. I go out back and look up. The heavens, embarrassed by gobs of stars. I strike a match to life, empower a cigarette and wait for the wind to come, then the rain, then the sun.

Then the fucking roosters.

A girl tests her echo against the mountain. A boy throws his tooth onto a roof and prays for a new one. An ancient woman with a hooked spine pummels mealies with a mortar and pestle. Later, she'll boil the powder into a thick porridge and eat with her hands. All I have is a bucket of chicken feet and heads. Walkie-talkies.

I hitchhike forty kilometers to Polokwane, roam its innocuous streets. Tswanas sell single Stuyvesants for two rand on the corner of Market and Kerk, opposite the taxi rank. Afrikaners wash their bakkies behind the electrified fences of Cycad Estates. This place is still a scab.

Walking faster now, as if I have a destination. 'These Are Days' by 10,000 Maniacs is stuck in my head. My fingernails have grown too long, beard as well. My reflection skips across shop windows, metamorphosing. I wish I could stop and stare but that takes something like courage. It's October. Where are the jacarandas?

David Poseidon

He loves running from tides,
spittle awash in whiskey and the dead hum
of cop cars underwater, a siren song.

Baby bullet exited his skull's ceiling,
a blowhole for daydreams to float out
alongside plankton and flashbacks.

He serves the Atlantic, loves the way
it sways its hips, how it swallows all.
He worships warships, counts sand.

There are sea ballerinas, delicate
as tiptoes, pirouetting to heartbeats,
ripping open their fuchsia gills

to invite him inside. But he ocean-crawls
with hermit crabs, shell-shocked. Sorry, girls.
He's busy. He's drowning. He has somewhere to be.

The Girl Who Broke New Ground

From my window I watch a girl
whip a white hula hoop
around her hips.
She's plump.
She's Saturn.
Her yellow skirt puffs
like a blowfish.
Her metal bracelets rattle.
The sky is silk and

falling.
She cracks the hoop
into semicircles.
Her skin becomes burlap.
Her mouth is bloody
from hunting squirrels.
She spins so fast
her thick, black braid
grows erect and she drills
herself straight to hell
where she puts on a parka
and says to the devil, 'Move over, pal.
There's a new bitch in town.'

Something is smudged
and I can't tell which:
my window or my world.

Skeleton Key

He rips out her spine to use as a walking stick,
struts outside, pokes sea glass and driftwood.
She slumps forward on the piano bench,
her nose pecks a key that unlocks the entire island.

The sour note sinks, a tsunami surges, belly flops
on the man who made her play 'Chopsticks'
then give head to the tick of a metronome.

She pushes her baby grand out of the bungalow
and into the Caribbean. Tiger sharks shred
the meat and spit out the ivories. They patter ashore.

She sidewinds the coast, collecting beached keys
in a basket. She stacks them, one by one,
up the length of her back until her head is moon-high
and she can catch a comet between her teeth.

Postmodern Housewife

She nearly kills her baby by uninstalling antivirus software.
She Skypes 911 but the robot speaks JavaScript, not English.
She renames the kid 404 Error, props him in a highchair.
She force-feeds him crushed moonbeams from a satellite dish.

She hacks into her daughter, unlocks her thighs.
She resets the V-chip, teleports her to the prom.
She live-tweets the war on Mars until her stream dies.
She refreshes her homepage, www.postmodernhousewife.com.

She runs low on battery power, cries, blows a fuse.
She inserts modems into her ears; dial tones calm her.
She plugs her arteries into a speaker, bleeds the blues.
She refrigerates a slab of meteor left over from dinner.

She crashes to bed. Rubbing his hard drive, hubby's in the mood.
She disconnects, downloads a dream and slips into sleep mode.

Grace

She loves only two things more than me: a gold dog called Oprah
and a medicine cabinet. As a young girl, she conquered
whooping cough but her throat is still full of gravel. She grinds
out sentences like 'Growin' up, we didn't have no pot to piss in!'
and 'Nothin' ain't never easy!' Freckles splatter her face, a Pollock.

She relies on clouds, names them, insists they're ancestors.
Cumuli—wide-hipped and jovial—are paternal grandparents;
wispy and thinly veiled, cirrus clouds are definitely from her
mother's side.

She's not crazy; she studied psychology at university. During the
day, she answers calls at a crisis center. Strangers dial from
mobile phones threatening to fall from ledges and she always
knows what to say: inflatable phrases that cushion the jumpers
just before they paint the pavement red.

Her name's Grace. We collided at a 24-hour convenience store this
morning, 2:30. We turned into the medical supplies aisle at the
same time. I was buying condoms, being optimistic. Bundled in
her arms were a bottle of aspirin, gauze and a bag of razors. She
looked like she always does—like she'd been crying. 'Do you
know what it's like to have a pocketful of sleeping pills in a city
that never sleeps?' she said, folding herself into my peacoat.
'Actually, yeah,' I said, but her question was rhetorical and she
wasn't listening.

At the checkout, she crawled into her enormous purse, spelunking for her wallet. All she could find were a pashmina, Sexton's *Love Poems* and fingernail polish. As the cashier silently judged her, I swiped my debit card for both of us, but Grace already had thundered through the automatic doors into the street. When she finds her wallet next week, she'll pay me back in promises and we'll be cool.

The Nobody

My subway stop is outside on an elevated platform. Beneath a shrug of moon, I waited for the J train with the usual salad of straphangers: four Bloods, an Orthodox Jew, a gaggle of boricuas, a drag king.

LaWasha and LaDrya, whose parents own a laundromat, were there, as was Miguel, whose abuelo runs the bodega with opened milk and dusty fruit. A hipster octopus stood with a ukelele, Ray-Bans, a Polaroid, *On the Road*, coconut water, a pack of American Spirit, a hemp tote, and her daughter, Matilda Clementine, in each arm.

And, of course, the humdrum of folks with featureless faces no one has ever looked at…they were there, but who cares?

Manhattan's skyline eyed all of us from a distance. The Chrysler, Empire State and World Trade—socialites blemished in diamonds, rolling on Molly, counting their bars of gold—became tall witnesses when a nobody fell onto the tracks.

The J came quickly and flattened him. The conductor screamed directives but all I could hear was something primal. A yelp punching through trachea. The fireworks of a 20-year-old child exploding. And the screech of metal on rail.

He had a face. It tried to reach heaven but got lodged in hell. Maybe he deserved it. Maybe I'll see him there.

Bainbridge Street

Early morning, the rats are awake. Cold air hugs like a step-mom.
January's jacked the bling from trees. Trash bags—black, plastic
Santas—slump curbside as brownstones sleep standing up. Soon,
police cruisers will be replaced by garbage trucks, then school
buses. Car alarms will duet with jackhammers. For now,
everyone's still tucked away, swashbuckling nightmares—
everyone but the lady in the wheelchair. She's singing Shakira,
chain-smoking, speeding down the middle of the street to greet
daybreak first.

Songbird

In the island's westernmost village hides The Monster: a drinking hole where real men reel men. Flimsy wrists and flying fists, it's every man for herself.

The crowd is a mixer of young men muscular as grasshoppers and older men in Levi's, flaunting big bulges—their wallets. Every Thursday evening, I enter through the exit, scan the bar and top the nearest stool. I don't order a drink, never dance. Just bird-watch.

He perches, right knee bent, boot flat against a stone wall. He looks old enough to have seen the raid with his own eyes. He wears black trousers, a white undershirt and a double-breasted maroon jacket. Strands of ashen hair are tucked behind his ears. Clumps of mascara, crow's feet, hooked nose.

Moving only his lips, he mouths the lyrics to every song the deejay plays. Eighties synth hits, saccharine pop from '98, disco diva classics—he synchs every word without feeling any of them. Sometimes the mirror ball casts a matrix of stars onto his vacant face. Aimless in ascent, but neither lost nor fading. He'll have his own stories when he lands.

Memory Hits

A finger painting: boy,
blue face, yellow neck, green grin,
waving at an orange house,
red mom in the chimney waving back,
purple sunshine filling the void.

Tonight, he prowls Alphabet City,
catwalking Avenue B in Lycra and lace,
rogue smudges of rouge on his cheeks,
ripped pantyhose and the pull of chandeliers,
one hung from each lobe, pavement scraping
their golden arms, clinks of crystals smashing,
pinging into gutters, no cabbies stopping
to haul him to Bed Stuy at this hour.

When the walkabout memory hits, he halts,
kicks off his stilettos, pivots. The painting.
Trot turns to a dead sprint, he's panting,
rushing blindly through crosswalks,
running drag routes through the grid,
sweating through drugstore make-up,
careening towards the orange house.

World Wide Web

I

I know a man with two first names, two last names and 365 faces. He once used an instructional video on YouTube to build a nitroglycerine bomb. 'No focus the destruction,' he told me. 'Look, I create, no?'

We met in a locker room in Caracas. I'd just bench-pressed a set of encyclopedias; he'd carved ice cubes into his abdomen. His smile revealed icicles for incisors. We mangled Spanglish in a Jacuzzi for an hour before slinking to the sauna's underbelly. There, I melted him to my size.

We were 27. I told him I was originally from New York City, which was a lie. He called me a gringo then asked what Americans call people from Venezuela. I said, 'Mexicans,' and neither of us laughed.

I told him I was the editor of the world's most boring magazine. He told me he was a doctor and that he saved a life last week. I asked if he could save mine. He pretended to think, slowly shifting shapes. He had a year's worth to choose from.

II

Balancing on longitude like a tightrope, I searched the Americas.
When I reached Toronto, the CN Tower fell flaccid. I took twine
from my knapsack and continued spinning my web.

Tied an enormous knot around the skyscraper, connected it to a
sign marking Bloor Street, unraveled for a mile, made a loop
around a flagpole flying the Maple Leaf, meandered through
Chinatown, wove the line through a bike rack opposite a Tibetan
eatery, crisscrossed it around tree trunks on U of T's campus,
bound it to a random statue then asked a valet at the Hilton to
hold the tail end. Tightly.

At 4:25pm, he was snagged. Fidgety, unshaven, surprised to see
me. It had been nearly two years since Caracas.

He took me to a corner café. We traded eyeballs and stared at
each other. Far-sighted, the both of us. We spoke in our second
languages, resting our mother tongues. He told me who he'd
been dating and I gave him the finger under the table. I told him
of my sister's cancer and he promised to cut it out.

In his studio on Richmond Street West, he said, 'We shouldn't do
this,' as I indented him into his double bed. 'Wish we'd never
met,' I said, unbuttoning his flannel with my right hand, untying
our heartstrings with the left.

Underpoem

At the turn of the century, you loved my poetics,
how my tongue could flick a rhyme,
how it licked you.

Lately I hear you've fallen for mathematics,
how the systematic grunt work of matrices
makes you want to multiply.

I write in the same buttery language
that whispered to the visceral you
like a porcelain underpoem.

He communicates in geometrics and proofs;
to him you two are parallel lines,
to me we are a couplet.

You toss up radical signs like hurdles
but I leap over, long-legged,
racing towards the square root
of this diseased weed, buried
beneath my pretty please,
your thanks but no thanks.

I'll let you and Math return to your calculations,
but when you tire of scratch work,
remember us rolling on the floor, me on top,
slipping you a metaphor.

Painkiller

That bloodshot lady, throat coated
in quicksilver, her son, that queen
with Quaaludes, yeah I know them.

You could say I made them rich
before I wrote headlines
for their tombstones

and licked the marble to numb
my gums. Look at me: perfect
damage. My brain goes rat-a-tat-tat,

zoom-zip-zap. I can sell you this feeling.
You got my number. I'm that brown-eyed
failure with no fingerprints and a killer

smile, always here to help. Just ask.
I can write your headline, too,
and it will change your life.

Aftermath

We had a threesome with Him
on an apocalyptic morning after math class.
Choirboys had false teeth, sang a vulture hymn
backwards. Their black melodies stained glass.

He and I kissed beneath a crucifix. Cross-eyed,
you tongue-twisted an Apostle's Creed.
My synapses snapped like mousetraps and I
died, was reborn. Religion was what I needed
to kill so I Frankensteined an angel
from dirt, trapped it in a handful of daylight
then broke its neck. I measured the angle
and offered it up to Pythagoras. It was right.

You foxed away with Him to be his finest whore.
I put lipstick on my sad angel and learned 1 + 2 = 4.

Bazaar

Beneath the steeple a banner boasts: *Our 3rd Annual Charity Bizarre! January 21st! Basement of St. Agnes' Church!*

The misspelling goes unnoticed as parishioners, housewives and cutthroat senior citizens haggle over tricycles and garden gnomes, an ottoman, a broken Victrola—anything they don't need and won't use. An overwhelmed woman buys two left-foot galoshes. A boy hits his sister with his brand-new, used flute. Newlyweds get a bargain on a king-sized mattress with queen-sized sheets.

I rummage through a devout couple's collection of unusual boxes. All kinds—a mailbox shaped like a mallard, a hatbox from the Fifties, a jack-in-the-box to startle a child, an invisible box to trap a mime, a voice box to trap a scream. Next to me, a man in drag—maybe Father McClanahan—strikes the deal of the day, an unbeatable 2-for-1 offer on a box spring to plant the pop of Agnes and a lunchbox to hide her cherry in.

Meltdown

The night sky is a blackboard I fly
near on Thursday but Thursday's Thor's day.
A thunderbolt cracks my forehead, fries
my mind. I become a vegetable. I sputter clichés.
My verbs and subjects doesn't agree.

I orbit.

On Friday night, the moon's hungry.
It eats a smorgasbord then squeezes into a corset.
Earthlings snap back their necks to gawk
as it spews chewed stars. Faster than an astronaut,
I rocket to the blackboard with a stick of pink chalk.
I don't know whose skin I'm in as I connect the dots
of Orion, his collarbone, his love handles. I melt
down in front of him. On my knees, I unbuckle his belt.

Exposure

In a grove of twisted citrus trees, naked people thrash each other. They lust for the perfect combination. Men with horse thighs find women who spread like peacocks. Bodies clap in soil, pant in unison. They deep kiss until lips disappear and they're lapping a slit on a face. Everything tongues taste flows into mouths. They suck each other down, her navel then his. His nipples, the nape of her neck. His abdomen flakes like salmon, her breasts bust. They scoop out eyes like melon balls, swallow each other's throats. Skin sheds, exposing tender tendons. Intestines entangle, choke the life out of innards. Blood lubricates the slipping and pounding as thousands of pelvises collide, pulverizing flesh. Soon it's just bones raging on bones, rib cages shattering, femurs bashing like baseball bats.

On the outskirts of the grove, hidden cameramen hold their equipment and masturbate to what's left: a crop of hearts fucking like dogs.

The Hush

It happens on a May morning.
The grass, dewy as foreskin,
gym class outside.

Your instructor rocks a tight buzz.
A stopwatch on a cord flirts
with his camouflaged heart.

Ryan edges Randy—no one's surprised.
Keith and Chip run and run and run and
tie. Taylor sprains his ankle.

You race the nameless kid
who wishes you luck then beats you.
Your buddies bust their bellies and die
laughing.

'Newman!' Tully says. 'That homo
made you his bitch!' They heckle like jackals
into the locker room.

The kid with motor legs
faces a corner, changes
his shorts. You creep.

The hush.

A semicircle forms.

The kid turns.

He knows.

You think, 'Good race,'
but say, 'Fucking fag,'

and you know he won because he's used to being chased.

Williamette

Inside our father's womb,
my brother broils
for four and a half months.
Quasi-boy, undercooked
but unbreakable.

Umbilical cord of barbed wire,
wrought iron wrists, *Made in America*
branded on his bottom.

Backbone of Pittsburgh steel,
pigskin, lisp-proof tongue,
thunder in his hair.

Not one teardrop.

He grows into a quarterback
who grunts in huddles then launches
a Hail Mary just before a blindside tackle
plants his heart deep in Astroturf.

But me or Holden
will be open in the end zone
with Krazy Glue and deft hands
to complete the pass, win the Bowl
and harvest his heart, that
spit-shined, brazen-blue,
masculine muscle.

Embers

The man lacked three things: self-identity, survival skills and a killer instinct.

I led him to Diamondback River, where rapids unfurl over rock. He stood on the bank, peered into the water and saw his face for the first time. A ripple of Adonis.

He grew hungry. I showed him how to feed a line through a hole, knot it, then shank a hook into a night crawler. There'd be a pop of blood, I warned. I helped him lift the rod skyward and cast. He marveled at the arch. 'Adjust the slack. Wait 'til you get a bite.'

The red-and-white bobber soon sunk and, with an upward jerk of the rod, the hook pierced the lip of a rainbow trout. We pulled in our catch, watched it fuss on sand. We scaled it, filleted it and had dinner—as did the fish, its belly full of earthworm.

At midnight, I introduced him to the moon—deadpan, pockmarked, trustworthy. He was unimpressed. I told him I'd teach him how to build a fire if he could find kindling. He unzipped his jeans and mine and rubbed together the branches. Sparks, then a small blaze. He knelt, blew on it, then stepped back and let the flames take me. He slept by my warmth through the night.

In the morning, he revisited the river to see if he could smile any bigger.

Piñata

The morning sun lassos a ray around my neck and hangs me.

Parents blindfold their children, spin them three times, then slip oversized branches into their palms. 'Play nice,' they say, as the kids take turns whacking me. They send me swooping across the sky. Sometimes, when I'm hit from both sides at once, I'm sandwiched still.

By midday, parents tell their children to stop beating me with oversized branches. 'Aluminium drainpipes,' they recommend. They smack me raw. After several hours, the children's arms tire and they stop beating me with aluminium drainpipes.

Parents then grab their children by the ankles, tell them to stay stiff and use their kids to beat me.

Finally, I break. The neighborhood rejoices in the sun shower. They snatch all they can straight from the air and stuff their faces. They want me so bad I almost mistake it for love.

'Mmm, I got a failure tear!'

'Not as salty as my queer tear!'

'His ugly tear tastes like peppermint!'

Soon the moon, fat as a bull, charges the sun. The ray unravels from my neck and I fall to Earth. Empty, I smack concrete without making a thud. Up and down the street, kids suck puddles dry through straws.

My ulcers will crowd their pot bellies by sunrise.

Word Problem

Meghan, AJ, Mikey and Maria Esperanza organize a drug sale to raise funds for a new jungle gym at Cottonwood Elementary School. They bake weed into 60 double fudge brownies, load 20 grams of crack into makeshift pipes and align 40 grams of coke with a MasterCard Meghan stole from her mom. The fundraiser is a huge success at recess and their grand total should be $7,600. But AJ took 2 quick hits from a soda can, Mikey snorted 3 lines of nose candy through a one hundred dollar bill (which he kept) and Maria Esperanza devoured 8 brownies because she eats her feelings. Using the current street value of these drugs, calculate to the nearest dollar the total profit made by these young entrepreneurs then subtract the cost to incarcerate them until their eighteenth birthdays.

Answer: _____

Nové

He was born in a speeding taxi
during a blizzard so frigid
snow angels flew south.

Whizzing beneath red stoplights, the cab
slid on asphalt, slicked by black ice,
through a tunnel that unhinged its jaw.

Landmarks lashed past. A blur
of town hall, snippets of Main Street, flashes
of the courthouse and a porn shop.

His mother screamed like a Salem girl,
her legs wishboned in the backseat
as she puffed, pushed, popped.

The boy's first blanket was a floor mat
and he was nearly named after the cabbie,
Morris, but he reeked of vodka.

So she called her baby November.
Nové, a nickname. He grew up to be a doctor
or a race car driver or a poet. No one's sure.

He left home as a teen, believing he was
some broken boomerang flung into this
lame world on a whim, not meant to return.

And in some ways he was broken.
Flinchy, one leg longer than the other,
fearing heights, depths, the middle ground.

Now his mother spends her days peering out
windows, side-eyeing taxis, expecting one night
to hear a soft knock. The door is always unlocked.

En Route to Colombo

'...he sent me to London when I was 13. Boarding school, then LSE. Almost finished. Dating this hot Welsh girl. Can't complain. So yeah, what brings you to Sri Lanka? Just backpacking? You should head to the north. Beautiful beaches, people smiling from the time they wake up 'til the sun quits. Some land mines still, mind your step. Hey, you on Facebook?'

Row C, en route to Colombo. We've been fed mutton curry and slices of orange, given warm face cloths and cooling hand wipes by attendants in teal saris. Above the aquamarine Indian, peppered by the Maldives, the younger man beside me unpacks thoughts as if going to the same destination requires him to share where he's been. Eyes, skin and hair all hues of brown.

'...so yeah, anyway, I'm going home to bury him. He didn't like the government much so he fought. Newspapers called him a guerrilla so our family would joke, 'He's a Tiger, not a gorilla!' But to me he's just my dad, you know? Well, *was*. Shit, he could be bloody ruthless though. Once ripped a bloke's ear off. Did you know ears are detachable? If you...'

Lighthouse

Seems like yesterday we were stabbing little plastic boats with sticks of dynamite. I forget which of us said, 'You sunk my battleship,' but I remember the game was over and you backed the Cadillac down the driveway. I watched from the bay window as you drove to the end of our street and turned towards the wharf. You didn't check the rearview. I was eleven with the beard of a wise man.

None of that matters now—I'm spiraling up the 199 steps of Cape May lighthouse with a steel chain around my waist, an anchor hooked at the end. It clangs the helix of steps and shoots metallic chills up the lighthouse's spine. I reach the top landing and blink the light frantically. Can't you see my flailing, silhouetted arms? You've forgotten something!

But you remain at sea. And the links are digging so deeply into my hipbones, Dad, I think I may break in half.

Handsome

Twist of face, gnarled silver dollar
nostrils, oblong eyeballs snatched
from a funhouse. Dotted line inked
across your Adam's apple, thin skin
reads: *Cut here.* Unibrow, fivehead,
latticework of scars, tic-tac-toe.
Your mouth, a lipless gash,
your molars, urine-yellow cubes,
shadows slash from bye-bye
hairline to rotten potato chin.

You gnaw chain links,
emerge from the cellar,
crash through the front doors
of Wal-Mart. Shoppers scream.
You smile. Everyone says how nice
you probably are but nice
doesn't make you handsome.

If only everyday was a masquerade
or people stapled their eyelids shut
or firewomen extinguished the sun
so no one was forced to know you
are an ogre past your prime, boy
Gorgon, textbook disorder, how I see
myself.

Sorry I Asked

'Bad news,' my psychic says.
'The earth's flat
and your boyfriend's
boyfriend isn't you.
Doors are unhinging at every turn
of the knob and that bracing sky
you soared through as a child
has swapped places with hell...
your silver lining's en fuego!
Plus you're up for adoption
on eBay and the max bid's
a buck fifty and one sick goat.'

I give her my palm
and the news gets worse.

'Your love line's been erased
from giving too many hand jobs.
You thought that was your civic duty
like being a juror, a Good Samaritan,
or some bullshit artist who invents futures
for the foolish, the curious, the impatient.
Chill out. You think too much.'

The Diner

Dinnertime at Ocean Queen Diner on Route 70. Heart's 'Alone' leaks from the jukebox. Outside, lightning skins the sky stretched over the interstate. In a back booth with scarlet cushions, a bearded lady yawns. She's eating meatloaf and mash without a knife or fork. Her name is Rachel, Denise or Chuck.

I side-straddle a stool at the counter. A lazy Susan rotates blueberry pies, strawberry shortcakes and rubbery scones. I scan the menu, written in Esperanto, and order chicken fingers and a black coffee. The world's strongest waitress, Corinne, Robin or Tyson, says, 'No coffee tonight, kiddo. Just bathwater.' I ask for a tall glass and she brings me the whole tub.

At the cash register, conjoined twins argue over the check. Paul and Pat, Mike and Matt or This and That, they're attached at the hip. Eventually, they decide to split it.

Through the vestibule, I see the tallest man this side of the Metedeconk in the parking lot. On stilts, he's 24'9'. He's leaning against a telephone pole, his head between the wires, rudely slurping the last of a milkshake. On his shirt, a sticker reads: *Hello! My name is Atlas, Hercules or Dominique.*

When my supper arrives, a baby grandfather with a tin voice pokes me in the flank and screeches, 'Who do you think you are? You don't belong here. Get the hell out of our town!'

He's the ringleader, a full-time joker. 'Just kidding!' he says. 'We've been waiting for you! Welcome home, Bill, Bill or Bill! Is it really you?'

Closing

Shuffle of slippers on tile,
scrub of wet bristle on tooth,
fireplace snacking on logs,
earnest dog's yawn and stretch,
pull on and zip up of jeans,
dead bolt's reassuring click.

Muffled crunch of the closing
car door, weight of tires rolling
over road, muted commute to Brick
Hospital, droplets from bag to tube
to vein, beeps and blips of a machine
trying to save a body it just met.

Stifled breathing, disquieting
doctor talk, a forced joke,
a nervous laugh, 'Want anything
from the canteen? Diet Coke?
A muffin?' an unexpected turn,
a sudden squeeze, not yet.

Finally

From the man, finally,
hostility's banished, not like
dust feathered from a bare shelf
or a smudge wiped from glass
with one swipe of terry cloth,

but rather a 32-year surgery —
robotic arms incising and extracting
cancerous pacts between tumors
and traumas, rumors and dramas,
scares and scars until every shard
of shrapnel entombed in tissue,
sunk in skin from explosions of life,
is carefully, completely removed.

Only now may the man quit
cataloguing his self-combustions
and release his fluorescence —
those grotesque fits of happiness,
embarrassingly sincere smiles,
his wingspan, the warmth.

Secret Song

Held a conch to my ear,
heard the earth of Etta,
opened a mail bomb,
discovered a love letter,
peered into a pistol,
saw kaleidoscopic twirls,
burst someone's bubble,
became terrorist to the world,
sent up a smoke signal,
was texted straight away,
watched you sleep,
realized all men are afraid.

author photo © Nathan William Meyer

Bill Trüb has spent much of his life waiting to board airplanes. He grew up in the beach town of Brick, New Jersey, completed a BA with honors from Moravian College in Pennsylvania, earned an MA with distinction from Cardiff University in Wales, served in the United States Peace Corps in rural South Africa, taught teenagers in inner-city Brooklyn and currently works as a lecturer of English at Wenzhou-Kean University in China. Bill is 32 years old and openly male.